Animal Lives

Food and Feeding

Kimberley Jane Pryor

MACMILLAN
LIBRARY

First published in 2010 by
MACMILLAN EDUCATION AUSTRALIA PTY LTD
15–19 Claremont Street, South Yarra 3141
Reprinted 2011

Visit our website at www.macmillan.com.au or go directly to www.macmillanlibrary.com.au

Associated companies and representatives throughout the world.

Copyright © Kimberley Jane Pryor 2010

All rights reserved.
Except under the conditions described in the *Copyright Act 1968* of Australia
and subsequent amendments, no part of this publication may be reproduced,
stored in a retrieval system, or transmitted in any form or by any means,
electronic, mechanical, photocopying, recording or otherwise, without the
prior written permission of the copyright owner.

Educational institutions copying any part of this book for educational purposes
under the Act must be covered by a Copyright Agency Limited (CAL) licence
for educational institutions and must have given a remuneration notice to CAL.
Licence restrictions must be adhered to. Any copies must be photocopies only,
and they must not be hired out or sold. For details of the CAL licence contact:
Copyright Agency Limited, Level 15, 233 Castlereagh Street, Sydney, NSW 2000.
Telephone: (02) 9394 7600. Facsimile: (02) 9394 7601. Email: info@copyright.com.au

National Library of Australia Cataloguing-in-Publication entry

Pryor, Kimberley Jane, 1962–
   Food and feeding / Kimberley Jane Pryor.
   ISBN: 9781420271621 (hbk.)
   Pryor, Kimberley Jane, 1962– Animal lives.
   Includes index.
   For primary school age.
   Animals—Food—Juvenile literature.
591.53

Publisher: Carmel Heron
Managing Editor: Vanessa Lanaway
Editor: Paige Amor and Georgina Garner
Proofreader: Tim Clarke
Designer: Ben Galpin
Page layout: Ben Galpin
Photo researcher: Lesya Bryndzia (management: Debbie Gallagher)
Illustrator: Ben Spiby
Production Controller: Vanessa Johnson

Printed in China

Acknowledgements

The author and the publisher are grateful to the following for permission to reproduce copyright material:

Front cover photograph of corkwing wrasse, courtesy of Photolibrary/Age Fotostock/Marevision Marevision.

Kelvin Aitken/ANTPhoto, **25**; N.H.P.A./ANTPhoto, **20**; iStockphoto.com/Leo Coombes, **28**; iStockphoto.com/Hazlan Abdul Hakim, **24**; iStockphoto.com/Marco Kopp, **14**; iStockphoto.com/Paul Lemke, **29**; iStockphoto.com/Hugh MacDougall, **27**; JupiterImages Unlimited/Photos.com, **13**, **19**; Photolibrary/Age Fotostock/Marevision Marevision, **4**; Photolibrary/Animals Animals/Michael Dick, **12**; Photolibrary/David Courtenay, **17**; Photolibrary/Georgie Holland, **16**; Photolibrary/Oxford Scientific (OSF)/Nick Gordon, **22**; Photolibrary/Oxford Scientific (OSF)/Friedemann Koster, **23**; Photolibrary/Pacific Stock/James Watt, **15**; Photolibrary/Photo Researchers/Dr Merlin Tuttle-BCI, **18**; Photolibrary/Fritz Polking, **9**; Shutterstock/Ewan Chesser, **8**; Shutterstock/dragon_fang, **10**; Shutterstock/Marsha Goldenberg, **21**; Shutterstock/Johann Hayman, **30**; Shutterstock/Cathy Keifer, **11**; Shutterstock/Four Oaks, **26**; Shutterstock/szefei, **5**.

While every care has been taken to trace and acknowledge copyright, the publisher tenders their apologies for any accidental infringement where copyright has proved untraceable. Where the attempt has been unsuccessful, the publisher welcomes information that would redress the situation.

For Nick, Thomas and Ashley

Contents

Animal lives	4
Food and feeding	5
Diagram: Food web	6
A food web shows what different animals in a community eat.	
Preying on large animals	8
Some animals kill and feed on prey much larger than themselves.	
Swallowing small animals whole	10
Many animals swallow small animals in one huge gulp!	
Dining on the relatives	12
Some animals dine on their own kind!	
Feasting on fish	14
Both land and sea animals feast on slippery fish.	
Snacking on small sea animals	16
Many animals eat small sea animals that are poisonous, hard-shelled or spiny.	
Eating insects	18
Many animals eat huge numbers of insects.	
Swallowing eggs	20
Some animals feed on bird and reptile eggs.	
Sipping blood	22
Vampires feed on the blood of the living!	
Chewing leaves and grasses	24
Many animals browse on leaves or graze on grasses.	
Licking fruits and flowers	26
Fruits and flowers are sugary treats for some animals.	
Crunching nuts and seeds	28
Nuts and seeds can contain tasty food.	
Believe it or not: Eating dung	30
Glossary	31
Index	32

Glossary words

When a word is printed in **bold**, you can look up its meaning in the glossary on page 31.

Animal lives

Animals face many challenges in their lives. From the moment they are old enough to look after themselves, they have to work hard to survive. They must search for food. They need to escape from hungry **predators**. They have to find or make safe homes so they can shelter from the weather and hide from danger.

When they become adults, animals must attract mates so they can have young. Some animals travel to faraway **breeding** grounds to have their young. After they hatch or are born, many young need to be protected and cared for until they, too, are old enough to survive on their own.

One of the challenges that a corkwing wrasse faces is to search for food, such as shrimps, to eat.

Food and feeding

All animals must find, obtain and eat food. An animal needs to eat food to stay alive and grow. The first thing the animal needs to do is to find the right type of food – and then it needs to get the food. Getting the food can be difficult because most plants and animals do not want to be eaten!

Different types of food

Different animals eat different types of foods. Some animals, known as **herbivores**, eat plants or plant foods, such as fruits and nuts. Some animals, known as **carnivores**, hunt, kill and eat other animals. **Omnivores** are animals that eat both plant and animal foods.

Did you know?

In this book you will find out about:
- snakes that swallow animals that are larger than their own heads
- frogs that gobble their relatives
- bats that sip the blood of the living
- beetles that eat **dung**.

A hornbill is a herbivore that searches rainforest treetops for fruits to eat.

Diagram: Food web

Southern Ocean food web

In a Southern Ocean food web, tiny floating plants, called phytoplankton, make food using energy from the Sun. Some animals eat the phytoplankton and some animals eat other animals such as **krill**.

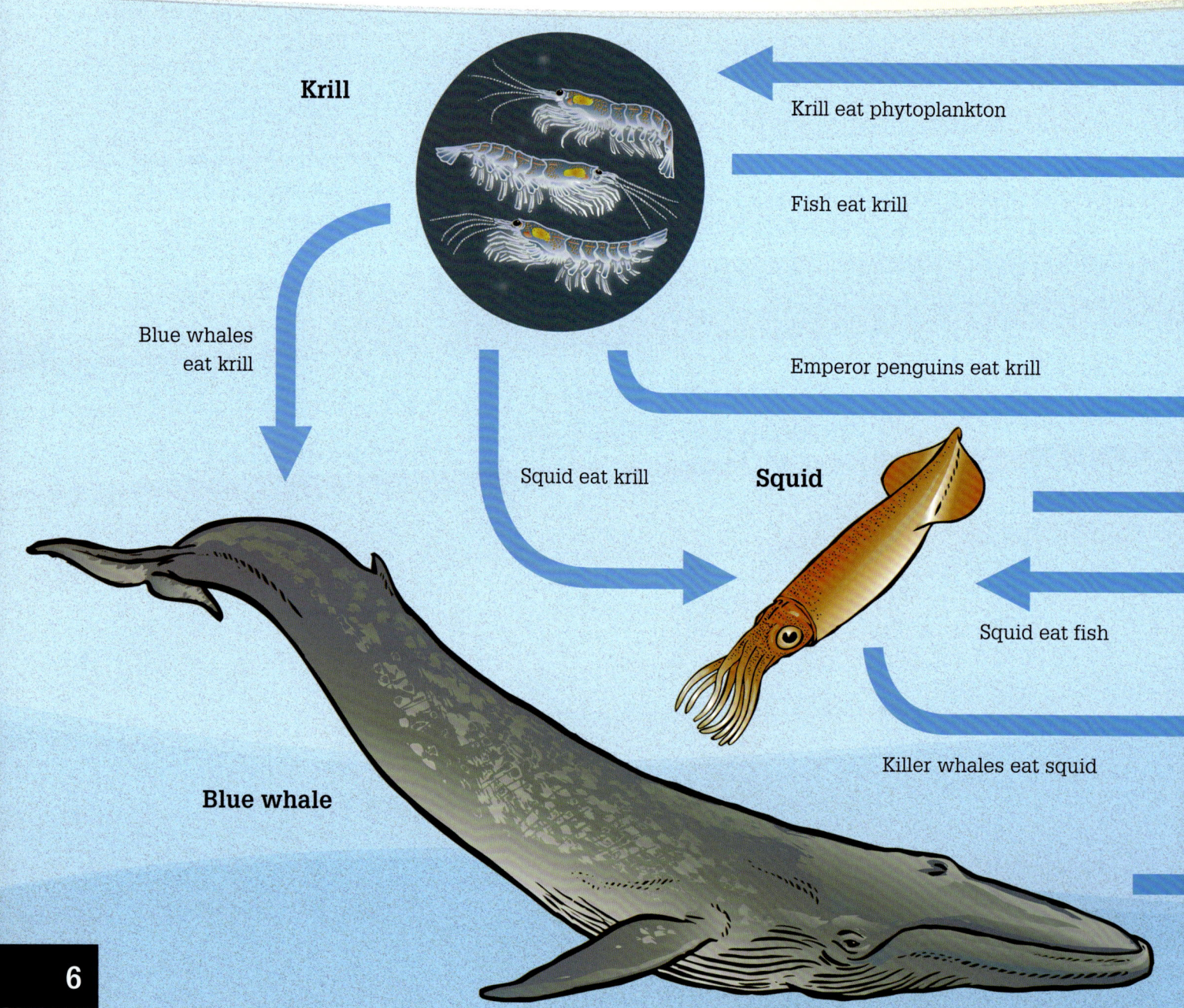

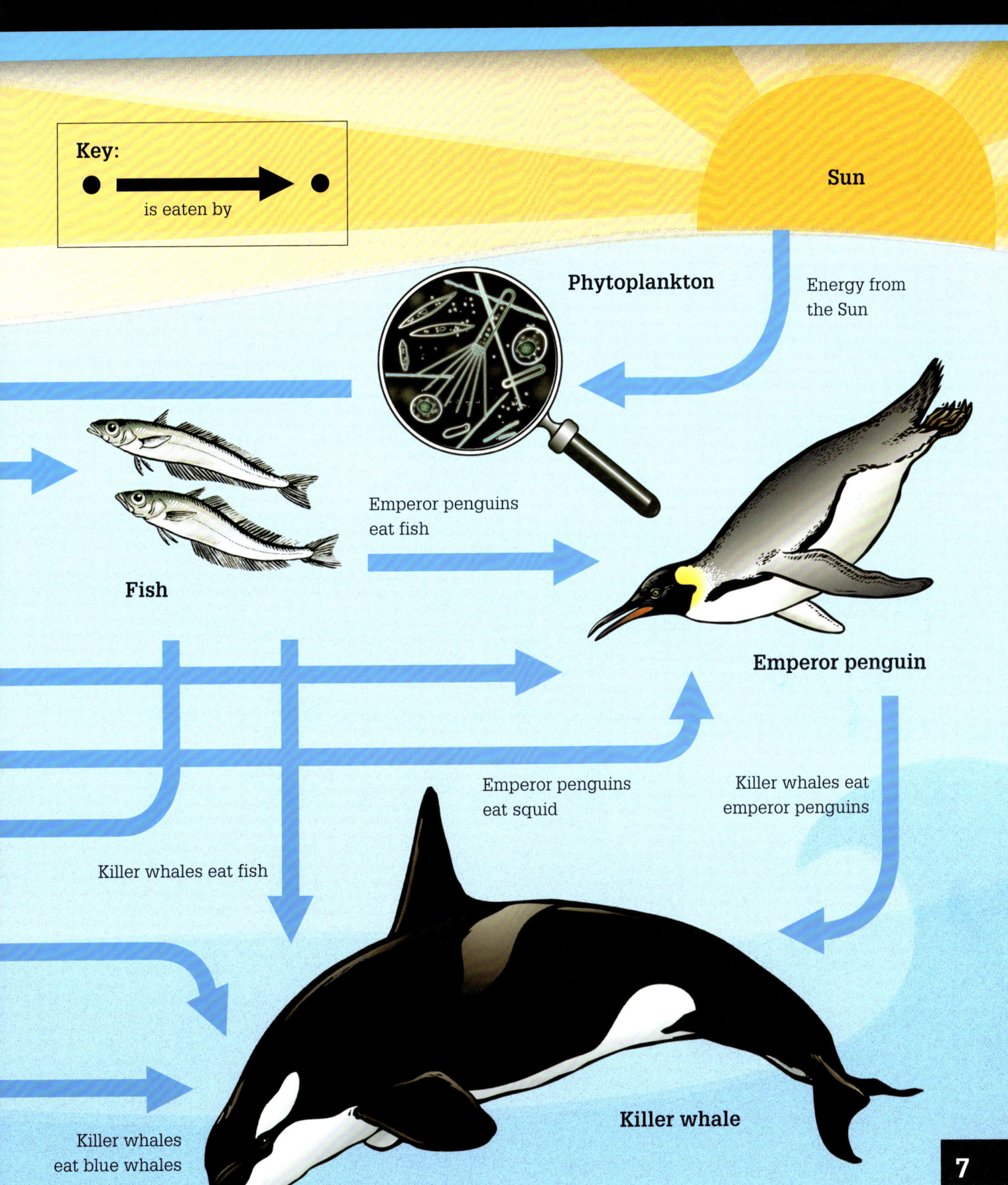

Preying on large animals

FACT FILE

Type of animal: mammal

Head and body length: 1.3 to 1.9 metres

Habitat: forests and bushland

Distribution: Africa and Asia

Main foods: crabs, fish, **reptiles**, birds, rodents, hares, warthogs, monkeys, baboons and antelopes

Leopard

A leopard is a fierce **predator** that feeds on any animal it can catch and kill.

Leopards usually live and hunt alone. They are **nocturnal**, and hunt by stalking their prey in long grass. A leopard pounces on its prey and kills it with a swift bite to the throat. It can kill animals that are much larger and heavier than itself because it has a huge skull with powerful jaws.

Did you know?

Leopards are excellent climbers. They sometimes hide in trees and drop onto prey passing below.

A leopard often drags its prey up a tree so it cannot be stolen by lions or hyenas.

 **Some animals kill and feed on prey much larger than themselves.**

A large rock python usually swallows an impala by starting with the head.

Did you know?

A python can stretch its mouth around an entire large animal! It can do this because its upper jaw is not fused to its skull. It can also move its lower jawbones far apart.

Python

A python mostly hides and then attacks its prey. It swallows its prey whole. It can even swallow animals that are larger than its own head, such as crocodiles and antelopes!

Pythons use a method of killing prey called 'constriction'. After catching an animal, a python quickly coils its body around it. The python then slowly tightens the coils to stop the animal's breathing. The pressure of the coils can stop the animal's blood flowing or break its bones.

 **FACT FILE**

Type of animal: reptile

Length: 1 to 10 metres

Habitat: rainforests, woodlands, grasslands and deserts

Distribution: Africa, Asia and Australia

Main foods: lizards, crocodiles, birds, rats, goats, pigs and antelopes

Swallowing small animals whole

A brown owl snatches a mouse, carrying it away before swallowing it whole.

Did you know?
Several hours after eating, an owl **regurgitates** a pellet made of **prey** parts, such as scales, feathers, beaks, fur, teeth, claws and bones.

FACT FILE

Type of animal: bird

Length: 13 to 70 centimetres

Habitat: rainforests, forests, woodlands and grasslands

Distribution: every continent except Antarctica

Main foods: insects, fish, frogs, snakes, birds, mice, rats, shrews, voles and possums

Owl

An owl is a **nocturnal** bird of prey. It eats small animals, such as mice and rats, by swallowing them whole.

Owls are superb hunters because they have good eyesight and excellent hearing. They can fly silently because they have special wing feathers. Some owls fly over their hunting grounds and swoop on prey. Others drop from a perch onto their prey.

Many animals swallow small animals in one huge gulp!

Lizard

A lizard eats mostly small animals. Some lizards have special teeth to help them eat particular types of animals, such as earthworms or snails.

Lizards sometimes race up and down trees or walls to catch their prey. They usually grab a small animal and swallow it whole. A lizard eats a snail by crushing the shell, swallowing the soft body and then spitting out the pieces of shell.

FACT FILE

Type of animal: reptile

Length: 6 centimetres to 3 metres

Habitat: rainforests, forests, woodlands, grasslands, deserts and beaches

Distribution: every continent except Antarctica

Main foods: insects, spiders, snails, worms, plants and dead animals

Did you know?

A lizard flicks out its tongue to gather smells from the air. This is how it senses and tracks small animals.

A leopard gecko can swallow a cricket whole.

Dining on the relatives

FACT FILE

Type of animal: reptile

Length: 4 metres

Habitat: rainforests, forests and grasslands

Distribution: Asia

Main foods: other snakes, lizards, **mammals** and eggs

King cobra

A king cobra hunts and kills other snakes. It eats both **venomous** and non-venomous snakes.

King cobras hunt by day. A king cobra flicks out its forked tongue to help it sense and track **prey**. It kills the prey by biting it and injecting **venom**, before swallowing it headfirst! The prey is just the right shape to fit inside the king cobra's body.

Did you know?
A king cobra can go without food for months after eating a large meal.

A king cobra's favourite food is other snakes.

12

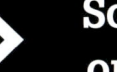  **Some animals dine on their own kind!**

A bullfrog catches and eats a smaller frog.

Did you know?

When a frog swallows, it pulls its eyeballs inwards to help push the food down its throat.

Frog

A large frog often eats other frogs. It eats frogs that are smaller than itself because it swallows the food whole.

A frog eats living, moving prey. It flicks out its long, sticky tongue, catches the prey and pulls it into its mouth. A frog spits out anything that is bad tasting or poisonous. It sometimes uses its hands to stuff food further into its mouth.

 **FACT FILE**

Type of animal: amphibian

Length: 1 to 30 centimetres

Habitat: rainforests, forests, deserts and swamps

Distribution: every continent except Antarctica

Main foods: insects, spiders, worms, lizards, snakes, birds, mice and bats

13

Feasting on fish

A bald eagle holds a slippery meal in its **talons**.

Did you know?

When a bald eagle grabs a fish that is too heavy to lift, the eagle is dragged into the water. It then uses its large wings to swim to shore.

⬇ FACT FILE

Type of animal: bird

Length: 90 to 108 centimetres

Habitat: near rivers and lakes, and along coasts

Distribution: North America

Main foods: crabs, fish, turtles, snakes, other birds, small **mammals** and dead animals

Bald eagle

A bald eagle feeds mostly on fish. It hunts for its own fish or steals fish from other fishing birds, called ospreys.

Bald eagles stand on perches or fly over water to look for fish. They swoop feet first and seize fish with their curved talons. A bald eagle grips a fish tightly and flies to its nest or a perch to eat its meal.

14

 **Both land and sea animals feast on slippery fish.**

Humpback whale

A humpback whale eats fish. It opens its huge mouth and scoops up the fish.

Humpback whales use a method of fishing called 'bubble-net feeding'. Several humpback whales work together and blow bubbles while swimming in a circle towards the water surface. Fish get trapped inside the circle of bubbles and swim to the surface of the water. The humpback whales then lunge at the fish, scoop them up and gulp them down.

 **FACT FILE**

Type of animal: mammal

Length: 12 to 16 metres

Habitat: near the coasts of seas and oceans

Distribution: worldwide in seas and oceans

Main foods: krill, plankton and fish

Did you know?
Using bubble-net feeding, each humpback whale can catch up to 1361 kilograms of fish per day!

Humpback whales work together to catch large schools of fish to eat.

15

Snacking on small sea animals ....

FACT FILE

Type of animal: reptile

Shell length: 82 centimetres

Habitat: coral and rocky reefs, and seagrass beds

Distribution: warm parts of the Indian, Pacific and Atlantic oceans

Main foods: sponges, sea snails, soft corals, sea jellies, fish, seagrasses and seaweeds

Hawksbill turtle

A hawksbill turtle feeds mostly on small, colourful sea animals called sponges.

Hawksbill turtles swim around coral and rocky reefs and over seagrass beds in search of food. They prefer to eat certain types of sponges. A hawksbill turtle uses its sharp, hawk-like beak to pick sponges out of cracks and crevices. Young hawksbill turtles feed on floating plants and animals near the ocean surface.

Did you know?

A hawksbill turtle can eat some poisonous sponges and not get sick. It can also eat sponges that contain hard, glass-like rods.

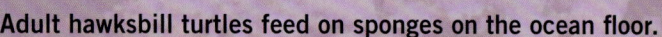
Adult hawksbill turtles feed on sponges on the ocean floor.

 **Many animals eat small sea animals that are poisonous, hard-shelled or spiny.**

A sea otter snacks on a spiny sea urchin.

Did you know?
A sea otter uses its senses of sight and touch to help it find food. It touches objects with its whiskers and front paws.

Sea otter

A sea otter dives to the ocean floor to look for small sea animals to eat. It stays underwater for up to five minutes.

Sea otters pull crabs and sea snails off seaweeds, and dig up clams. They also use small rocks to hammer small sea animals off rocks. They put food in loose skin folds in their armpits and then swim to the surface of the water. A sea otter floats on its back and uses a rock to smash open any sea animals with shells.

 **FACT FILE**

Type of animal: mammal

Head and body length: 76 to 120 centimetres

Habitat: seaweed forests

Distribution: Pacific Ocean

Main foods: crabs, sea snails, clams, sea urchins, limpets and fish

Eating insects

A Hildebrandt's horseshoe bat is a type of microbat that finds and catches cicadas while flying.

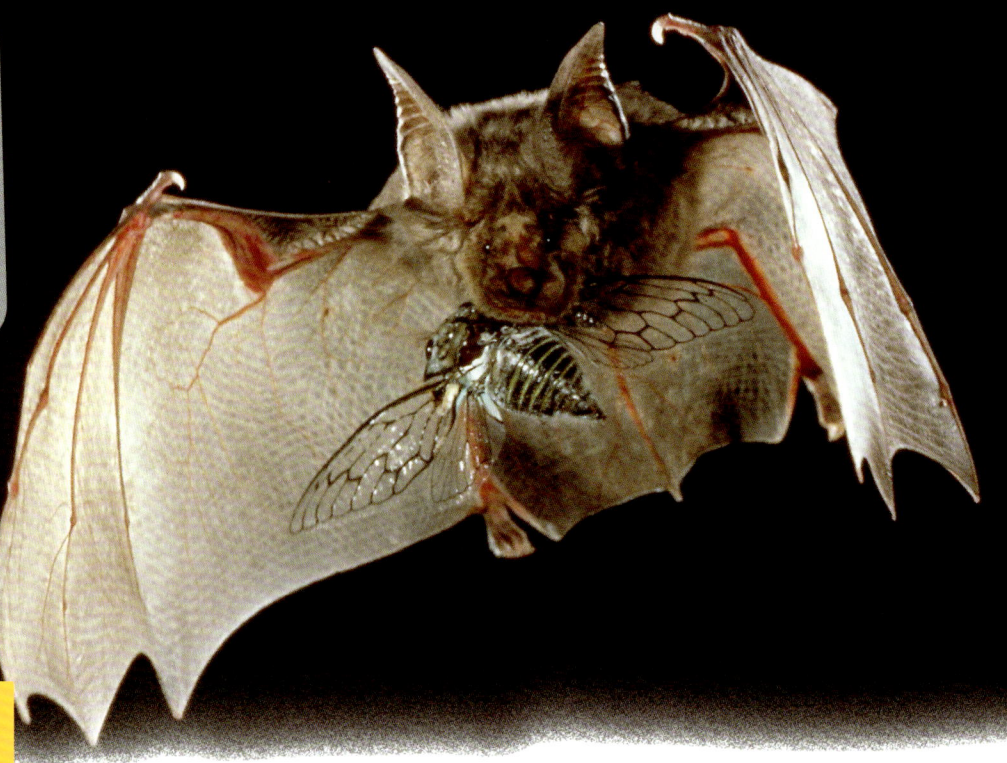

Did you know?
A microbat can catch hundreds of insects in an hour. It can eat one half of its body weight in insects in one night!

FACT FILE

Type of animal: mammal

Head and body length: 3 to 13 centimetres

Habitat: caves, crevices, tree hollows and under bark

Distribution: every continent except Antarctica

Main foods: mosquitoes, flies, moths, beetles, bugs, dragonflies, wasps and cockroaches

Microbat

A microbat feeds mostly on flying insects. It uses **echolocation** to help it find and catch food.

As it flies, a microbat sends out sounds from its nose or mouth. The sounds hit objects and bounce back to the microbat as echoes. The echoes tell the microbat what and where the objects are. The microbat finds out if any of the objects are tasty insects.

Many animals eat huge numbers of insects.

Giant anteater

A giant anteater gathers insects with its long snout and sticky tongue.

Giant anteaters use their keen sense of smell to help them find food. They dig up or tear open ant nests and termite mounds with their strong front claws. A giant anteater then licks up the insects with its 60-centimetre-long tongue!

FACT FILE

Type of animal: mammal

Head and body length: 90 to 120 centimetres

Habitat: forests, woodlands and grasslands

Distribution: Central and South America

Main foods: ants, termites and small grubs

Did you know?

A giant anteater can stick out its tongue 150 times a minute. It can eat 30 000 ants in a single day!

Giant anteaters tear open logs with their strong claws so they can eat the insects inside.

Swallowing eggs

Egg-eating snake

An egg-eating snake eats nothing but eggs. It has stretchy skin, **moveable** jaws and tiny teeth to help it fit a whole egg into its mouth.

When it is hungry, an egg-eating snake pulls an egg into its mouth. It moves the egg into its throat and breaks the eggshell using the sharp spines on its neck bones. The liquid inside the egg flows into the snake's stomach. The snake then **regurgitates** the hard pieces of eggshell.

FACT FILE

Type of animal: reptile

Length: 76 centimetres

Habitat: forests

Distribution: Africa

Main foods: eggs

Did you know?

A slender egg-eating snake can swallow an egg that is much bigger than its head! It can do this because its bones are loosely connected and its skin is very stretchy.

An egg-eating snake can swallow a large chicken egg whole.

 **Some animals feed on bird and reptile eggs.**

A red fox sometimes steals and eats eggs from henhouses.

Did you know?
A red fox feeds mostly on insects and fruits in summer. It feeds mostly on mice, rabbits, birds and dead animals in winter.

Red fox

A red fox eats all kinds of foods, including eggs from bird and turtle nests.

Red foxes are **nocturnal** and hunt for food at night. They use their excellent senses of sight and smell to find eggs. Red foxes eat the eggs straightaway or carry the eggs away and store them to eat later.

FACT FILE

Type of animal: mammal

Head and body length: 57 to 74 centimetres

Habitat: forests, grasslands and deserts

Distribution: Africa, Europe, Asia, Australia and North America

Main foods: eggs, insects, fruits, mice, rabbits, birds and dead animals

21

Sipping blood

Vampire bats often feed on the blood of sleeping horses.

Did you know?
A vampire bat drinks about one half of its body weight in blood each night!

 **FACT FILE**

Type of animal: mammal

Head and body length: 9 centimetres

Habitat: caves, mines and tree hollows

Distribution: North, Central and South America

Main foods: blood

Vampire bat

A vampire bat feeds only on blood. It makes a cut in an animal with its razor-sharp teeth and then laps up the flowing blood.

Vampire bats are **nocturnal** and hunt after dark. A vampire bat finds a sleeping bird or mammal and lands beside it. It then removes a thin slice of the victim's skin with its teeth. The vampire bat's saliva keeps the victim's blood flowing. The vampire bat laps up the blood for about 30 minutes!

Vampires feed on the blood of the living!

Vampire finch

A vampire finch feeds on blood when it cannot find other foods. It also feeds on plant seeds and the eggs of seabirds.

The home of a vampire finch is very dry for most of the year. When food and water become scarce, a vampire finch turns to blood! It lands on the tail of a seabird and pecks at the skin. When the seabird starts to bleed, the vampire finch sips the blood.

FACT FILE

Type of animal: bird

Length: 15 centimetres

Habitat: Darwin and Wolf islands

Distribution: Galapagos Islands

Main foods: blood, seeds and eggs

Did you know?

Vampire finches sometimes line up behind a seabird to wait for a turn to sip its blood.

Vampire finches sometimes feed on the blood of seabirds, such as masked boobies.

23

Chewing leaves and grasses

FACT FILE

Type of animal: mammal

Height: 5.5 metres

Habitat: woodlands and grasslands

Distribution: Africa

Main foods: leaves, twigs, bark, flowers, seed pods and fruits

Giraffe

A giraffe has a very long neck, which helps it eat leaves on the tops of tall trees.

Giraffes prefer to eat the leaves of thorny acacia trees. A giraffe strips the leaves off a branch by closing its mouth around the branch, then pulling its head back. It has tough, flexible lips and a long, thick tongue that protect it from the sharp thorns.

Did you know?

A giraffe often eats more than 30 kilograms of leaves in one day. It does not need to drink every day because the leaves contain water.

A giraffe eats leaves that other animals have no hope of reaching.

24

Many animals browse on leaves or graze on grasses.

A dugong stirs up a cloud of sand as it feeds on seagrasses on the ocean floor.

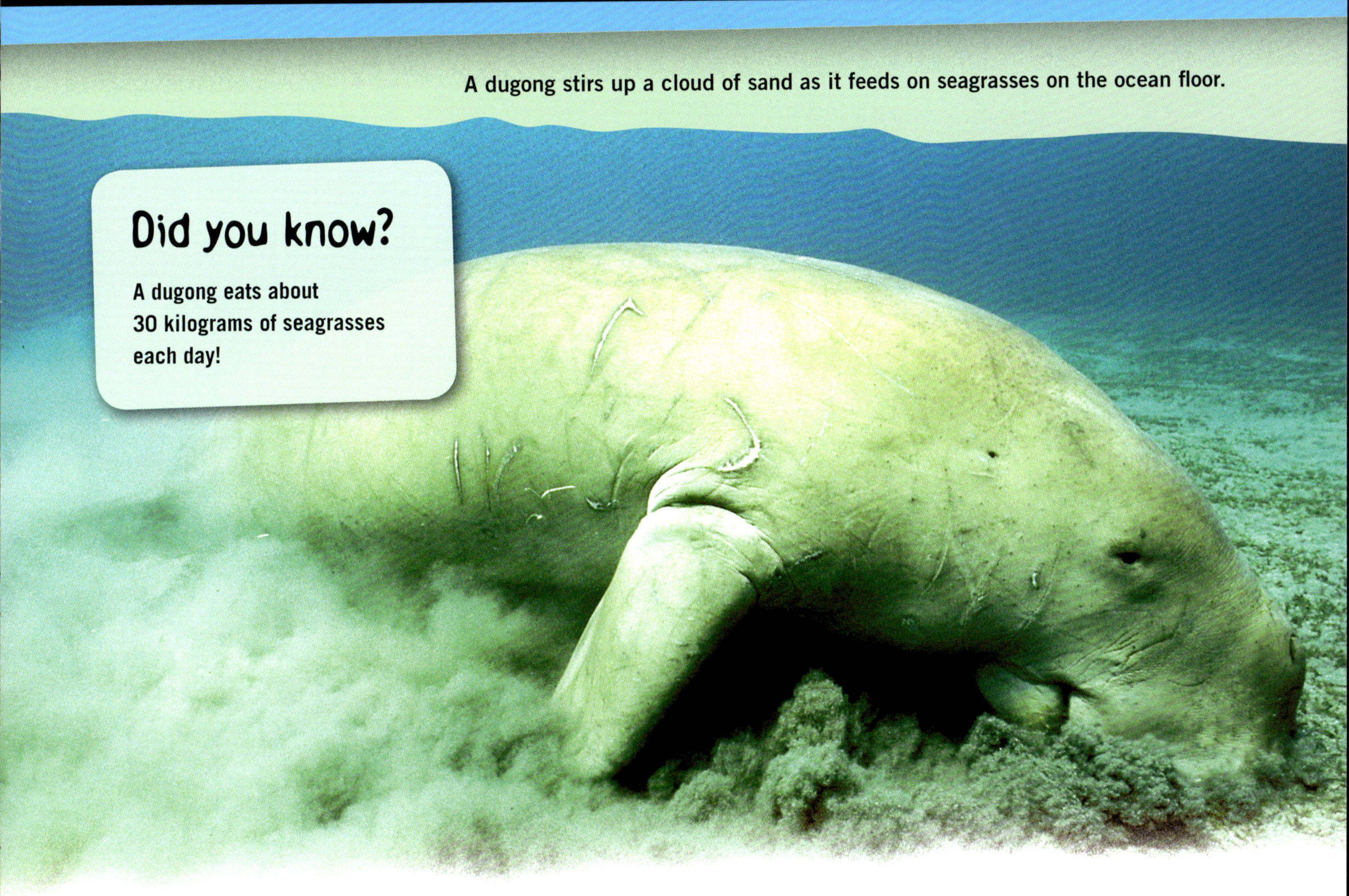

Did you know?
A dugong eats about 30 kilograms of seagrasses each day!

Dugong

A dugong grazes on plants called seagrasses, which grow in salt water. It prefers some types of seagrasses to others.

Dugongs use their flippers to 'walk' along the ocean floor when they feed. They leave feeding trails behind them as they move from place to place. A dugong uses the bristles on its upper lip to help it find and grasp seagrasses. It often pulls up a whole plant with its snout.

 **FACT FILE**

Type of animal: mammal

Length: 3 metres

Habitat: shallow coastal waters

Distribution: Indian and Pacific oceans, and the Red Sea

Main foods: seagrasses

Licking fruits and flowers

A fruit bat often drapes itself around a fruit while it is eating.

Did you know?

A fruit bat has excellent senses of sight and smell. It uses them to find ripe fruits and fresh flowers at night.

 **FACT FILE**

Type of animal: mammal

Head and body length: 6 to 40 centimetres

Habitat: rainforests, forests, mangrove swamps and paperbark swamps

Distribution: Africa, Asia and Australia

Main foods: fruits, nectar and pollen

Fruit bat

A fruit bat feeds on plant juices. Larger fruit bats feed mostly on fruits. Smaller fruit bats usually feed on nectar and pollen.

Fruit bats fly out from their camp after sunset to feed in fruiting and flowering trees. When eating a fruit, a fruit bat chews it and swallows the juice. It spits out the fibre and large seeds. When feeding from a flower, a fruit bat licks the nectar with its long tongue. It also licks up any pollen that sticks to its fur.

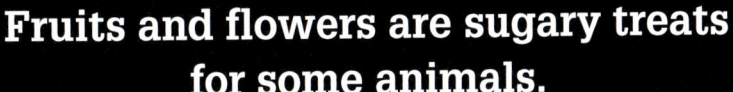
Fruits and flowers are sugary treats for some animals.

Rainbow lorikeet

A rainbow lorikeet feeds mostly on nectar and pollen. It has tiny hairs on the tip of its tongue to help it gather nectar.

Rainbow lorikeets fly as far as 50 kilometres in search of food. They often gather in large noisy groups in flowering trees, chattering and screeching as they move from flower to flower. They sometimes hang upside-down to feed from flowers.

FACT FILE

Type of animal: bird

Length: 30 centimetres

Habitat: rainforests, forests, woodlands and heathlands

Distribution: Asia and Australia

Main foods: nectar, pollen, soft fruits, insects and grain crops, such as sorghum and maize

Did you know?
A rainbow lorikeet feeds in the early morning and late afternoon. It only needs to feed for two to three hours each day.

Rainbow lorikeets sometimes feed on the fruits of an umbrella tree.

Crunching nuts and seeds

FACT FILE

Type of animal: mammal

Length: 10 to 90 centimetres

Habitat: forests, woodlands, deserts and **tundra**

Distribution: Africa, Europe, Asia, and North and South America

Main foods: nuts, insects, bird eggs, tree **sap**, plant shoots, flowers, fruits, seeds, pine cones and mushrooms

Squirrel

A squirrel feeds on nuts and other foods. It stores food for winter by burying it or hiding it in trees.

When a squirrel wants to open a hard nut, it takes the nut to a safe place. It holds the nut with its hands and front top teeth, then it scrapes its bottom front teeth across the nut. This makes a small hole, which the squirrel gradually widens until it can get at the soft food inside.

Did you know?

Squirrels use their sense of smell to find buried nuts. However, sometimes they forget where they have buried their nuts, and the nuts grow into trees!

A red squirrel crunches on a peanut.

Nuts and seeds can contain tasty food.

An American goldfinch cracks a cone flower seed in its strong, thick beak.

Did you know?
A young finch cannot crack ripe seeds, so its parents **regurgitate** seeds and insects for it to eat.

Finch

A finch feeds on both the partly ripe and the ripe seeds of grasses and weeds. It cracks the seeds with its stout beak.

Finches feed with the same or different types of finches, on or near the ground. Some finches hop along the ground with their feet together as they search for fallen seeds. Others balance on plant stalks and peck at the seed heads.

FACT FILE
Type of animal: bird

Length: 10 to 27 centimetres

Habitat: forests, woodlands, grasslands and **heathlands**

Distribution: every continent except Antarctica

Main foods: seeds and insects

29

Believe it or not:
Eating dung

A **dung** beetle rolls its valuable dung ball away from other dung beetles that might steal and eat it!

Did you know?
A female dung beetle lays her eggs in dung balls. When the young hatch, they eat the dung!

FACT FILE

Type of animal: invertebrate

Length: 5 to 30 millimetres

Habitat: forests, grasslands, deserts and farmlands

Distribution: every continent except Antarctica

Main foods: dung, mushrooms, and rotting leaves and fruits

Dung beetle

A dung beetle feeds partly or entirely on dung. Some dung beetles attach themselves to larger animals and wait for the dung to appear!

Dung beetles use their sense of smell to find piles of dung, which they then use to make dung balls. The dung balls are sometimes larger than the dung beetles. The dung beetles bury dung balls to use later for food or for raising young.

Glossary

amphibian	an animal that spends the first part of its life living in water and the second part of its life living on land	**plankton**	floating plants and animals
breeding	having young	**pollen**	the yellow powder in flowers
carnivores	animals that eat meat	**predators**	animals that hunt and kill other animals for food
dung	poo	**prey**	animals that are hunted and caught for food by other animals
echolocation	sending out sounds and listening to the echoes to sense objects	**regurgitates**	brings swallowed food up again to its mouth and spits it out
heathlands	land covered by low shrubs called heath	**reptile**	a creeping or crawling animal that is covered with scales
herbivores	animals that eat plants	**sap**	the sticky juice inside plants
invertebrate	an animal without a backbone	**talons**	the sharp claws of a bird of prey
krill	small, shrimp-like sea animals	**tundra**	a treeless Arctic plain with mosses, lichens and small shrubs
mammal	an animal that feeds its young with its own milk	**venom**	a type of poison
moveable	able to be moved	**venomous**	contains a type of poison called venom
nectar	the sweet liquid inside flowers		
nocturnal	active at night		
omnivores	animals that eat plants and meat		

Index

A
Africa 8, 9, 20, 21, 24, 26, 28
amphibians 13
Asia 8, 9, 12, 21, 26, 27, 28
Atlantic Ocean 16
Australia 9, 21, 26, 27

B
bald eagles 14
bats 5, 18, 22, 26
beetles 5
birds 10, 14, 21, 22, 23, 27, 29
blue whales 6–7

C
carnivores 4, 5, 6–7, 8, 9, 10, 11, 12, 13, 14, 15, 17, 18, 19, 20, 22
Central America 19, 22
corkwing wrasses 4

D
dugongs 25
dung beetles 30

E
egg-eating snakes 20
emperor penguins 6–7
Europe 21, 28

F
finches 23, 29
fish 6–7, 14, 15
frogs 5, 13
fruit bats 26

G
Galapagos Islands 23
giant anteaters 19
giraffes 24

H
hawksbill turtles 16
herbivores 5, 6–7, 24, 25, 26, 30
hornbills 5
humpback whales 15

I
Indian Ocean 16, 25
invertebrates 30

K
killer whales 6–7
king cobras 12
krill 6–7

L
leopards 8
lizards 11
lorikeets 27

M
mammals 6–7, 8, 14, 15, 17, 18, 19, 21, 22, 24, 25, 26, 28
microbats 18

N
nocturnal animals 8, 10, 18, 21, 22, 26
North America 14, 21, 22, 28

O
omnivores 5, 11, 16, 21, 23, 27, 28, 29
owls 10

P
Pacific Ocean 16, 17, 25
phytoplankton 6–7
predators 4, 8
prey 8, 9, 10, 11, 12, 13
pythons 9

R
rainbow lorikeets 27
red foxes 21
Red Sea 25
reptiles 9, 11, 12, 16, 20

S
sea otters 17
shrimps 4
snakes 5
South America 19, 22, 28
squid 6–7
squirrels 28

T
teeth 10, 11, 20, 22, 28
tongues 11, 12, 13, 19, 24, 26, 27

V
vampire bats 22
vampire finches 23

W
whales 6–7, 15